Snap books™

Crafts

Greeting Card Making

Send Your Personal Message

by Deborah Hufford

Capstone press

Mankato, Minnesota

Snap Books are published by Capstone Press,
151 Good Counsel Drive, P.O. Box 669, Mankato, Minnesota 56002
www.capstonepress.com

Library of Congress Cataloging-in-Publication Data
Hufford, Deborah.
  Greeting card making: send your personal message / by Deborah Hufford.
    p. cm. — (Snap books crafts)
  Includes index.
  ISBN-13: 978-0-7368-4385-0 (hardcover)
  ISBN-10: 0-7368-4385-X (hardcover)
  1. Greeting cards — Juvenile literature. I. Title. II. Series.
  TT872.H84 2006
  745.594'1 — dc22   2005006899

Summary: A do-it-yourself crafts book for children and pre-teens on
greeting card making.

Editors: Thea Feldman; Deb Berry/Bill SMITH STUDIO
Illustrators: Lisa Parett; Roxanne Daner, Marina Terletsky and Brock Waldron/Bill SMITH STUDIO
Designers: Roxanne Daner, Marina Terletsky, and Brock Waldron/Bill SMITH STUDIO
Photo Researcher: Iris Wong/Bill SMITH STUDIO

Photo Credits: Cover: (girl) MedioImages/Getty Images & Richard Hutchings Photography; 5 Digital Vision/Getty Images;
7 Corel; 8 PhotoDisc; 9 (r) Corel Stock Photo Library (l) PhotoDisc; 10, PhotoDisc; 13-14 PhotoDisc;
15 Corel; 16 (all), PhotoDisc; 17 (br, br & c) PhotoDisc; 18 (all) PhotoDisc; 19 Alamy Images;
20 (bl) Artville; 23 (bc) PhotoDisc ; 25 White Cross Productions/Getty Images; 26 (bl) PhotoDisc;
27 (cl) White Cross Productions/Getty Images; (bl) PhotoDisc; 32 Courtesy Deborah Hufford.
All other photos, Richard Hutchings Photography.

1 2 3 4 5 6 10 09 08 07 06 05

Table of Contents

CHAPTER 1 You've Got Mail 4

CHAPTER 2 Folded Fun 6

CHAPTER 3 Say It with Style 8

CHAPTER 4 Pretty Party Pop-up 10

CHAPTER 5 Walk on the Wild Side 14

CHAPTER 6 Very Fine Valentine 18

CHAPTER 7 Mosaic Magic 22

CHAPTER 8 A Photo Finish 24

Fast Facts 28

Glossary 30

Read More 31

Internet Sites 31

About the Author 32

Index 32

Go Metric!

It's easy to change measurements to metric! Just use this chart.

To change	into	multiply by
inches	centimeters	2.54
inches	millimeters	25.4
feet	meters	.305
yards	meters	.914
ounces (liquid)	milliliters	29.57
ounces (liquid)	liters	.029
cups (liquid)	liters	.237
pints	liters	.473
quarts	liters	.946
gallons	liters	3.78
ounces (dry)	grams	28.35
pounds	grams	453.59

CHAPTER 1

You've Got Mail

E-mail may be fast, but a handmade card will last.

The Internet has made it quick and easy to send greetings around the world. But nothing can beat the thrill of getting a greeting card in the mail. And just think how touched your friends and family will be to get handmade cards you took the time to make yourself.

REMEMBER!

Safety First

Look for this box throughout this book. It's where you'll find safety tips for each project. Remember, safety first, and fun will follow.

You can send a greeting card for almost any reason at all. Most greeting cards are either seasonal (sent for holidays) or everyday (sent for birthdays, to say "thank you," as a "get well," and more). These are the top greeting card occasions.

Whatever the occasion, you'll find plenty of fun ideas in this book to make your very own handmade cards.

1) Christmas
2) Birthdays
3) Valentine's Day
4) Anniversaries
5) Get Well
6) Friendship
7) Sympathy
8) Mother's Day
9) Easter
10) Father's Day

CHAPTER 2

Folded Fun

Greeting cards are folded paper with feelings inside.

Have you ever gotten a really neat greeting card, like one with fancy folds or a pop-up? Paper can be cut and folded into an amazing number of different cards. Here are a few examples.

French fold

Paper is folded in half, then folded in half again.

Accordion fold

A long piece of paper is folded back and forth to make many **panels**, looking like an accordion.

Gatefold

Paper is folded to create two panels opening in the middle like double doors.

Pop-up

Cut-out paper shapes "pop up" when a card is opened.

CHAPTER 3

Say It with Style

No two cards are exactly alike.

Each card you make is a totally new statement about your feelings for the person who will receive it. So go ahead and express yourself.

To get started you'll need paper, a few materials, tools, and some **decorative** items.

You can use almost any kind and color of paper, including,

* construction paper
* wrapping paper
* **specialty papers**

You'll also need scissors, glue, a ruler, and crayons, markers, or colored pencils. See each project for materials needed for that craft.

This book is loaded with ideas for decorating cards with beads, buttons, and other cool stuff. So get ready to make lots of cards!

Cutting Edge
Some special scissors are designed to cut fancy edges like zigzags and curves.

REMEMBER!
Safety First
Never handle scissors by the blades. Use them carefully, and keep them closed when not in use.

White Craft Glue

CHAPTER 4

Pretty Party Pop-Up

Start the party early with this "inviting" card.

Get your guests excited before a party by sending them this eye-popping invitation.

Don't be surprised if your pop-up card is so much fun that your guests "pop up" early the day of your party!

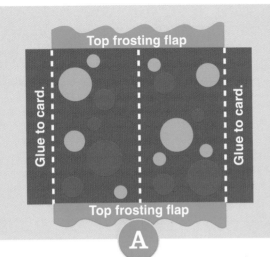

Top frosting flap

Glue to card.

Glue to card.

Top frosting flap

A

Glue flap to inside top of cake.

B

Here's what you need

* 2 sheets, any color 8½-inch
  by 11-inch heavy paper
  or **card stock**

* pencil

* ruler

* scissors

* markers, crayons,
  or colored pencils

* glue sticks

GLUE STICK

Here's what you do

1 Fold one sheet of paper in half to 8½-inches
by 5½-inches.

2 On the other sheet of paper, draw two patterns
similar to **Picture A** (cake) and **Picture B**
(candles). Each pattern should be about
4 inches by 3 inches. (Dotted lines on diagrams
show where the folds are.)

3 Color cake and candles as you like.

4 Cut out patterns.

5 Fold top and bottom curved "frosting" flaps
on cake forward (**Picture C**).

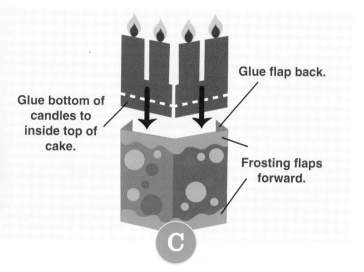

Glue bottom of candles to inside top of cake.

Glue flap back.

Frosting flaps forward.

C

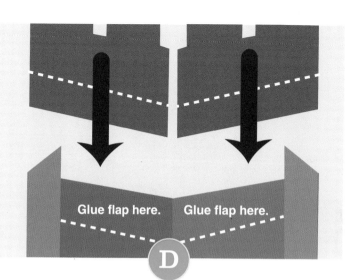

Glue flap here.　Glue flap here.

D

6 Glue bottom of candles to inside of cake. (**Picture C**).

7 Fold cake and candles down the middle.

8 Glue cake flaps on card. (**Picture D** shows a close-up of the back of the card where top part of the cake gets glued to bottom.)

Holiday Party Pop-Ups

Pop-ups also make great holiday cards. Here are some pop-ups you can try.

* heart with lace and red sequins

* shamrock with green glitter

* turkey with colored feathers

* jack-o'-lantern

13

CHAPTER 5

Walk on the Wild Side

Use nature's own "greetings" for your handmade cards.

Great card making materials are right outside your door. Just look in your yard or garden, or take a nature walk. (Always take care to pick plants only where allowed.) Consider these natural materials for making cards.

* flowers with stems and leaves
* single flower petals
* colorful autumn leaves
* tiny spring leaflets
* seeds
* grasses

Delicate plants and thin-petaled flowers work better than thick ones. Try pansies, petunias, morning glories, poppies, buttercups, or tiny daisies. Pick them from your garden or buy at a garden store.

Here's what you need

* fresh flowers, plants, or leaves
* paper towels
* heavy phone book
* any color 8½-inch by 11-inch card stock
* tweezers
* **decoupage glue**
* craft brush

Decoupage Glue

Here's what you do

1 Lay fresh flowers between paper towels.

2 Place phone book on top to press flowers for one to two weeks, until they stiffen and dry.

3 Fold card stock in half to 8½ by 5½ inches.

4 Arrange flowers on card front, trying different patterns.

5 Brush decoupage glue on paper, then use tweezers to glue flowers in place. Let dry 10 minutes.

6 Very gently brush decoupage over flowers and paper around them. Let dry.

7 Repeat Step 5 four times until flowers are completely coated.

Decked Out Decoupage

Plants aren't the only things you can decoupage. Make a card for a friend by gluing magazine pictures of her favorite things to the card's cover. Or try this great idea. Decoupage a picture of a person at the beach to a card's cover and glue a picture of your friend's face over it.

CHAPTER 6

Very Fine Valentine

> **Valentines aren't just for romance. They're for friends and family, too.**

In Victorian times, Valentines were made using a technique called **collage**. Collage materials can be just about anything.

* glitter
* beads
* photos
* stickers
* charms
* buttons
* pieces of old greeting cards
* pictures or words from magazines
* paper cut into shapes
* pressed flowers or plants
* ribbon
* lace
* yarn
* doilies

Here's what you need

* 8½-inch by 11-inch red construction paper
* 8½-inch by 11-inch pink construction paper
* 5-inch white, gold, or silver paper lace **doily**
* scissors
* white craft glue
* **glitter glue**
* any collage items listed on page 18

Here's what you do

1 Fold red construction paper in half to 8½-inches by 5½-inches.

2 Cut heart shape out of pink paper.

3 Cut heart shape out of doily, making it ½ inch smaller than pink heart all the way around.

4 Glue pink heart onto card, and glue doily heart onto pink heart.

5 Arrange collage items you like and glue to card.

6 Write something on the front in glitter glue, like the word "love" or someone's name.

Dream Card

Want to make a cool card for a friend? Fold a sheet of card stock into a gatefold (see page 7). Inside the card, glue a picture of something (or someone!) your friend dreams about, and write a special message. Next, glue the loop part of a frog knot (which you can buy at most crafts and fabric stores) to one "door" of the gatefold, and the knot part to the other. "Lock" the door by putting the knot through the loop. Write "Unlock Your Dreams!" in fancy letters on the cover. Your friend will be thrilled to get such a "dreamy" card.

CHAPTER 7

Mosaic Magic

Create mosaics from scraps in a snap.

Don't throw used fancy gift wrap away. Use it to make marvelous mosaics. Simply cut up some colorful papers and piece them together like a puzzle.

Here's what you need

* 8½-inch by 11-inch paper, any color
* scraps of wrapping or any color paper
* scissors
* pencil
* white craft glue

Here's what you do

1 Fold paper in half to 8½-inches by 5½-inches for body of card.

2 Draw a simple outline of something you like on the front of the card such as a flower or a star.

3 Cut paper scraps into ⅓-inch squares.

4 Arrange squares to fill in outline, being sure to leave a thin space between each square to create mosaic look.

5 Glue squares to card.

REMEMBER!

Safety First

Always keep scissors, glue, and sharp pencils away from young children.

Geometric Chic

Instead of a picture, draw a simple pattern like swirls, waves, or checkerboards and fill with brilliant pieces of colored paper.

White Craft Glue

CHAPTER 8

A Photo Finish

Turn a special snapshot into an instant keepsake.

Do you have a photo of yourself or a friend that you love? What about a special family photo or one of your favorite pet? No matter what's in the picture, you can turn it into a beautiful framed card.

Here's what you need

* 8½-inch by 11-inch card stock, any color
* pencil
* ruler
* scissors
* photo
* clear tape
* white craft glue
* decorative beads, buttons, lace, charms, or other items

Here's what you do

1 Fold paper into French fold (see page 6).

2 Mark card front with an "X" and unfold paper.

3 Using pencil and ruler, trace a 1-inch border inside cover panel and cut out center.

4 Place photo inside frame and tape back edges to back of frame.

5 Refold card.

6 Arrange decorative items of your choice around frame as desired.

7 Glue items to frame.

Old Fashioned Cards for Here and Now

For an old fashioned card, cut a round or oval frame by tracing an object with that shape. Center a black-and-white photograph in the frame and tape the back. Decorate with lace, buttons, ribbon, or charms.

REMEMBER!

Safety First

Remember to keep small items like beads, buttons, and charms away from young children and pets.

Fast Facts

House of Cards

The Hallmark Visitors Center in Kansas City, Missouri, has the largest collection of greeting cards in the world. They have more than 100,000!

Twinkle, Twinkle, Little Card

A new type of handmade card called a "Twinklecard" features Austrian crystals, pearls, and glass beads. They are placed in fancy designs on Japanese silk.

Love Lab

A science student in Rugby, England, created a special Valentine's Day card for his wife by growing millions of bacteria in the form of the words "I love you." How romantic!

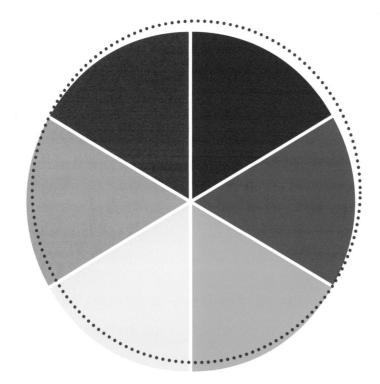

Color Wheel

When making greeting cards, color is key. This wheel shows how colors work with each other. The colors next to each other work together in harmony. Colors opposite each other have a stronger effect when used together because they have more contrast.

Glossary

card stock (KARD STOK) thick, stiff paper, like that used for postcards

collage (kuh-LAHZH) a picture made by gluing pieces of paper and other objects onto a card or sheet of paper

decorative (DEK-ur-uh-tiv) makes something prettier, as in "decorative beads" glued onto a card

decoupage glue (day-koo-PAHZH GLOO) glue that is brushed onto the entire surface of a card to attach pictures and objects to it; the glue then dries to make a clear coating

doily (DOI-lee) thin paper, usually round, with a pattern cut into it to make it look like lace

frog knot (FROG NOT) a type of "lock" made from fancy cord and usually used on Chinese clothing as buttons; available at most crafts and fabric stores

glitter glue (GLIT-ur GLOO) clear glue mixed with glitter that dries clear.

mosaic (moh-ZAY-ik) a picture or pattern made up of small "tiles" of paper or card stock

panel (PAN-uhl) a folded section of a card

specialty papers (SPESH-uhl-tee PAY-purz) pretty papers with special patterns, pictures, and colors

Read More

Emerson-Roberts, Gillian. *Card Book: Original Ideas for Handmade Greeting Cards, Step-by-Step.* United Kingdom: DK, 2001.

Hickey, Julie. *Quick and Clever Handmade Cards.* United Kingdom: David & Charles Publishers, 2004.

Suckling, Jan. *Making Cards in a Weekend: Inspirational Ideas and Practical Projects.* Cincinnati: North Light Books, 2000.

Internet Sites

FactHound offers a safe, fun way to find Internet sites related to this book. All of the sites on FactHound have been researched by our staff.

Here's how

1. Visit *www.facthound.com*
2. Type in this special code **073684385X** for age-appropriate sites. Or enter a search word related to this book for a more general search.
3. Click on the **Fetch It** button. FactHound will fetch the best sites for you!

About the Author

Deborah Hufford is a former staff editor of *Country Home* magazine and *Country Handcrafts* magazine, which featured a crafting section called "Kid's Korner." She was also the crafts editor for *McMagazine,* a magazine for McDonald's Corporation. Most recently she was the associate publisher for the country's two leading crafts magazines in beading and miniatures, *Bead & Button* and *Dollhouse Miniatures,* as well as the associate publisher for a book division of craft titles.

Index

accordion fold, 6

beads, 9, 18, 26
buttons, 9, 18, 26

card stock, 12
charms, 18, 26
collage, 18
craft brush, 16

decoupage glue, 16
dream card, 21

flowers, 14, 15, 16
framed photo card, 24
French fold, 6

gatefold, 7
glitter, 18
glitter glue, 20
grasses, 14

holidays, 5

lace, 18, 26
lace doily, 20

mosaics, 22, 23

nature, 14

petals, 14
photo, 18, 24, 26
pop-up fold, 7
pop-up card, 10-13
pressed flowers, 18

ribbons, 18

safety, 4, 9, 23
seeds, 14
snapshot, 24
specialty papers, 8
stickers, 18

tweezers, 16
twinklecard, 28

valentines, 18
Valentine's Day, 5
Victorian cards, 18

wrapping paper, 8

yarn, 18